DAVID MAXIM
UNSEEN PICTURES
1988-1996

David Maxim: Unseen Pictures
Copyright 1999 David Maxim
Library of Congress Catalog Card Number: 99-093398
ISBN 0-9673375-0-X

Published in San Francisco
Printed by AD Korea
adkor@netsgo.com

Cover: Detail of SHAMAN, 1993. pg. 19

DAVID MAXIM
UNSEEN PICTURES
1988-1996

With texts by Kenneth Baker and Anna Valentina Murch
Edited by Nicole Blunt

PREFACE

Since I am well acquainted with the artist's work, I was delighted when David Maxim asked me to make the primary selection of "unseen" pictures and edit their publication.

Among the works rarely seen by this artist, there were so many more that I would like to have chosen. Publication considerations precluded the many, however, and instead you see a presentation of only forty-eight of the most speculative and intense images resulting from the eight year period, 1988-1996. I focused on the artist's quasi-abstract works which are perhaps the most confrontational, and reflect an almost inflationary growth and vitality in Maxim's oeuvre during those years. I end with the first of his life-size figurative pictures, which serves as a convenient bridge to his next productive period, but lies beyond the scope of this book. Some of the developments apparent in these painting/constructions are considered in the catalog I assembled of the artist's drawings two years ago. There again, I was hard-pressed to hone a selection to only a few sheets from the draughtsman's very prodigious output.

While approximately two-thirds of the works represented here have never been exhibited, the remaining third have actually been seen, but only by a few attentive gallery goers in obscure venues, far away from the beaten path of the larger museums and other more usual exhibition spaces in the United States. Maxim's work is somewhat better known in Europe, having been prominently exhibited in various German art fairs of the 1980's, as well as being included in two large exhibitions of the Frankfurt Museum Für Moderne Kunst's permanent collection.

Nevertheless, Maxim's achievement remains, stunningly, a product of remarkable neglect. It is the purpose of this book to remedy the situation by simply presenting the work, albeit in poorly substituted book form, to a somewhat larger audience. If some faint magnitude of light is shed on the general obscurity that surrounds this artist, then this publication will have served a useful purpose.

I decided to dismiss the usual chronological order in this lean selection, and instead, have chosen to place the works in morphologically related groupings. This is because Maxim again picks up forms once abandoned, years later sometimes, as relationships intertwine and distill further and further. The editor hopes this method of presentation will show more clearly the relationships between seemingly disjunctive images, and reveal the working dynamics of ideas that brought the works about more clearly than would the usual chronological sequencing.

As of the printing of this book, all works are in the collection of the artist.

Nicole Blunt
Malibu, California, May 1999

AXIS OF THE WORLD, 1991
Acrylic on wood, canvas, twine,
metal fittings, excelsior.
45 x 34 x 6" (114.3 x 86.3 x 15.24 cm)

FREE WILL, 1991
Acrylic on wood, canvas, twine,
excelsior.
64 x 48 x 6" (162.56 x 121.92 x 15.24 cm)

8

ACT OF FAITH, 1992
Acrylic on wood, canvas, twine, metal
fittings, excelsior.
72 x 52 x 8" (182.88 x 137.16 x 20.32 cm)

Opposite Page:
WANDERING LIGHT, 1996
Acrylic on wood, canvas, rope, twine,
excelsior.
64 x 48 x 5" (162.56 x 121.92 x 12.7 cm)

DAVID, 1989
Acrylic on wood, canvas, net, burlap,
twine, metal fittings.
45 x 34 x 9" (114.3 x 86.36 x 22.86 cm)

THE LIMITS OF THE WORLD, 1988
Acrylic on wood, canvas, metal fittings,
rope, burlap, styrofoam.
84 x 64 x 20" (213.36 x 162.56 x 50.8 cm)

FOR SEVEN DAYS, 1991
Acrylic on wood, canvas, rope, twine,
metal fittings, styrofoam.
72 x 54 x 6" (182.88 x 137.16 x 15.24 cm)

Opposite Page:
COURSE OF EVENTS, 1993
Acrylic on wood, canvas, burlap, metal
fittings, rope, twine, styrofoam.
100 x 144 x 22" (254 x 365.76 x 55.88 cm)

BIRTH OF THE WORLD, 1992
Acrylic on wood, canvas, burlap, metal fittings,
rope, twine, excelsior.
100 x 144 x 15" (254 x 365.76 x 38.1 cm)

HOLE AND DISK, 1989
Acrylic on wood, canvas, rope, twine.
72 x 54 x 8" (182.88 x 137.16 x 20.32 cm)

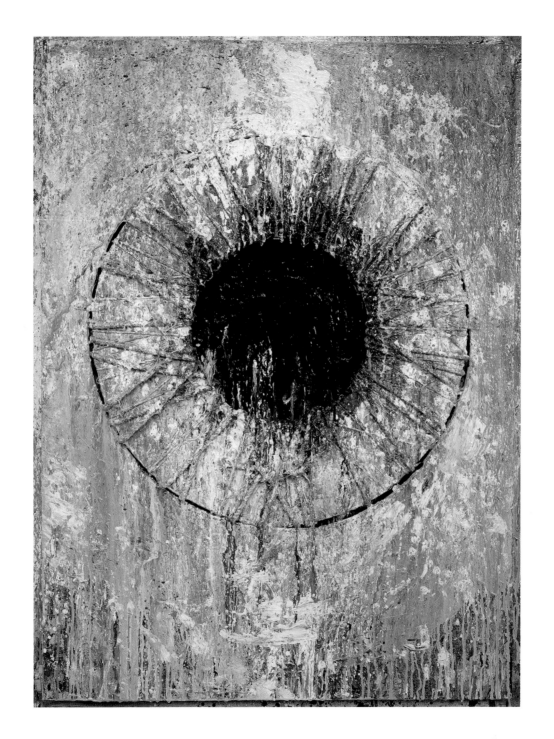

LOOK BACK, 1992
Acrylic on wood, canvas, rope, twine.
45 x 43 x 3" (114.3 x 86.36 x 7.62 cm)

TENDENCY TO SPIRAL, 1993
Acrylic on wood, canvas, barrel,
metal fittings, rope.
45 x 34 x 6" (114.3 x 86.36 x 15.24 cm)

SHAMAN, 1993
Acrylic on wood, canvas,
sheet metal vent.
64 x 48 x 8" (162.56 x 121.92 x 20.32 cm)

FORTUNE SMILES, 1992
Acrylic on wood, canvas.
64 x 45 x 4" (162.56 x 114.3 x 10.16 cm)

Opposite Page:
FREE WILL, 1990
Acrylic on wood, canvas, net,
metal fittings, rope, twine.
100 x 144 x 10" (254 x 365.76 x 25.4 cm)

THE ORACLE, 1989
Acrylic on wood, canvas, barrel,
rope, metal fittings, styrofoam.
100 x 72 x 21" (254 x 182.88 x 53.34 cm)

THE ORACLE, 1988
Acrylic on wood, canvas, barrel,
rope, metal fittings.
100 x 72 x 19" (254 x 182.88 x 48.26 cm)

THE GOD QUESTION, 1992
Acrylic on wood, canvas, net, twine,
rope, metal fittings.
100 x 72 x 22" (254 x 182 x 55.88 cm)

THE PRESENT IS PAST, 1991
Acrylic on wood, canvas, net, twine,
rope, metal fittings.
100 x 72x19" (254 x 182 x 48.26 cm)

THREADS OF THOUGHT, 1991
Acrylic on wood, canvas,
rope, string.
45 x 34 x 3" (114.3 x 86.36 x 7.62 cm)

THE SHAPE OF SELF, 1993
Acrylic on wood, canvas, net, string,
metal fittings.
45 x 34 x 5" (114.3 x 86.36 x 12.7 cm)

DETERMINISM, 1990
Acrylic on wood, canvas, burlap, metal
fittings, rope, twine, styrofoam,
life preservers.
100 x 144 x 18" (254 x 365.76 x 45.72 cm)

THE RIB, 1992
Acrylic on wood, canvas.
65 x 46 x 3" (165.1 x 116.84 x 7.62 cm)

TIME'S SPEED, 1990
Acrylic on wood, canvas, rope, twine,
metal fittings, cardboard, styrofoam.
64 x 48 x 10" (162.56 x 121.92 x 25.4 cm)

THE FOUR WINDS, 1990
Acrylic on wood, canvas, cotton bags,
twine, rope, metal fittings, styrofoam.
72 x 54 x 9" (182.88 x 137.16 x 22.86 cm)

MEANING IS THE BRIDGE, 1991
Acrylic on wood, canvas, cotton
bags, cardboard, rope, twine,
metal fittings.
44 x 35 x 7" (111.76 x 91.44 x 17.78 cm)

BEGINNING AND END, 1992-1996
Acrylic on wood, canvas, and string.
45 x 34 x 7" (114.3 x 86.36 x 17.78 cm)

THE PLOUGH, 1990-1992
Acrylic on wood, canvas, string, twine,
rope, metal fittings.
72 x 54 x 6" (182.88 x 137.16 x 15.24 cm)

THE CALL (from THE MIRACLES), 1995
Acrylic on wood, canvas, bedsheet,
cord, metal fittings.
96 x 65 x 20" (243.84 x 165.1 x 50.8 cm)

Opposite Page:
SHOUTS AND TRUMPETS
(from THE MIRACLES), 1991
Acrylic on wood, canvas, rope,
metal fittings.
100 x 144 x 20" (254 x 365.76 x 50.8 cm)

THE WISDOM OF SOLOMON, 1989
Acrylic on wood, canvas,
metal fittings, rope.
45 x 34 x 6" (114.3 x 86.36 x 15.24 cm)

THE OPEN PRESENT, 1992
Acrylic on wood, canvas, twine,
rope, metal fittings.
45 x 34 x 3" (114.3 x 86.36 x 7.62 cm)

THE UNIVERSE IS FLAT, 1992
Acrylic on wood, canvas, metal cage,
rope, cord, twine, metal fittings.
64 x 48 x 10" (162.56 x 121.92 x 25.4 cm)

Opposite Page:
THE CARTOGRAPHER, 1989
Acrylic on wood, canvas, burlap,
rope, twine, metal fittings, styrofoam.
84 x 128 x 13" (213.36 x 325.12 x 33 cm)

THE DEEPENING, 1990
Acrylic on wood, canvas, rope,
metal fittings.
72 x 54 x 16" (182.88 x 137.16 x 40.64 cm)

PAST AND FUTURE, 1991
Acrylic on wood, canvas, twine, rope,
metal fittings.
72 x 54 x 20" (182.88 x 137.16 x 50.8 cm)

THE ONTOLOGIST, 1989-90
Acrylic on wood, canvas, rope, twine,
metal fittings, styrofoam.
100 x 144 x 20" (254 x 365.76 x 50.8 cm)

RING, 1992
Acrylic on wood, canvas, twine,
cord, metal fittings.
45 x 34 x 5" (114.3 x 86.36 x 14.83 cm)

Opposite Page:
NOT ALONE, 1992
Acrylic on wood, canvas, rope,
metal fittings.
45 x 68 x 4" (114.3 x 172.72 x 10.16 cm)

PATRIARCHY, 1991
Acrylic on wood, canvas, basket, rope,
twine, metal fittings.
44 x 35 x 8" (111.76 x 88.9 x 20.32 cm)

ARMS OF SCIENCE, 1991
Acrylic on wood, canvas, burlap,
cardboard, rope, twine, metal fittings,
styrofoam.
199 x 72 x 25" (254 x 182.88 x 63.5 cm)

THE GNOSTIC, 1990
Acrylic on wood, canvas, cardboard,
burlap, rope, twine, metal fittings,
styrofoam.
72 x 54 x 20" (182.88 x 137.16 x 50.8 cm)

VEIL OF ILLUSIONS, 1991
Acrylic on wood, canvas, net,
cord, metal fittings.
44 x 35 x 6" (111.76 x 88.9 x 15.24 cm)

CAGED VISION, 1990
Acrylic on wood, canvas, wire screen.
45 x 34 x 4" (114.3 x 86.36 x 10.16 cm)

Opposite Page:
THE RADIUS OF EARTH, 1989-90
Acrylic on wood, canvas, burlap, rope,
twine, metal fittings, excelsior.
100 x 144 x 23" (254 x 365.76 x 58.42 cm)

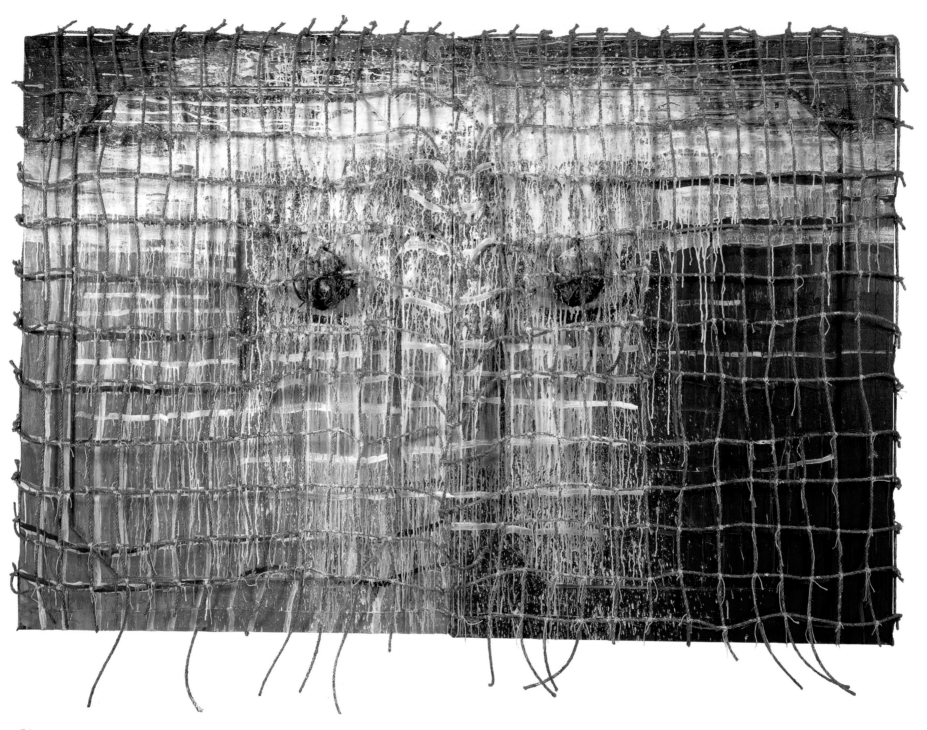

54

INFINITE VISION, 1993
Acrylic on wood, canvas,
cardboard, twine.
40 x 30 x 4" (101.6 x 76.2 x 10.16 cm)

Opposite Page:
GALILEO, 1996
Acrylic on wood, canvas, cotton bags,
rope, twine.
64 x 96 x 10" (162.56 x 243.84 x 25.4 cm)

THE DAYS TO COME, 1991
Acrylic on wood, canvas, burlap,
rope, twine, shirt, metal fittings,
excelsior.
100 x 72 x 24" (254 x 182.88 x 60.96 cm)

mysterious the drains always looked to me, down the black hole. So the picture has to do with the theme of gradual entropy that all of us — the whole universe — must finally conclude with. And that is the mystery of time's flow and pull. The paint's pulled like a vacuum into this realm that will contain everything. There are scientific speculations that would claim these infinite holes are necessary for a continuation into the next universe, continuing a Hindu-like cycle of death and rebirth.

Q. David, this painting, *Linear Thinking*, with the long slit in front of it, makes me have the feeling of constraint — restrictions of some sort.

A. Well, that's very apt. It is about constraint. It goes back to some lines I read from Shakespeare earlier this year that had implications for a number of pictures that I did with a slot. In one line from *Troilus and Cressida*, Shakespeare says something to the effect that the will is infinite, but the execution confined. This had great meaning for me and my experience as I see myself in the world. I might have the will to want to do anything and everything, but really I can only do a very small part of what I want to do. I am confined to who I am, to where I am, to my ability — and confined to the experience of my past as a starting point for my next activity in the future. This idea of restriction and limitation is expressed in the earlier painting, *The Limits of the World*. In *Linear Thinking* it is more a reference to the limits of myself. The paintings that I can do are only the paintings that *I* can do, and not someone else. See, the slot then is a symbol of my experience — and no matter what I do about it, it's linear — that is, I can't go back on it. It's also the keyhole through which I see the world and interpret it. I was using a paintbrush and squeegees and rags and sticks and pushing the paint back and forth, pushing it into that slot of my experience — to the edges of it. A lot of frustrated energy went into this. And this is how I see myself: a lot of the energy is frustrated and I would like to expand the limits of my ability to make a painting. I can do that to some small extent, but not nearly to the extent my will prefers.

Q. And all the drips and the surface and the layers on the other side of the slot, is that more…

A. Yeah. Well the other side of the slot, you see, has canvas that is free of paint because the flow of paint has been stopped by the wood surface over most of it. So the canvas is protected by the wood, rather like a helmet. If you continue the metaphor of a helmet, then the slot is seen at eye level. So the entire picture is a head and the slot is the opening for the eyes to see out from. The underlying soul-structure of the picture is hidden, it's been protected from other possible experiences — the other artists I might have been, or the other artists that are. Or the part of me that no one else can see and which is the part of me I only get inklings of when I am in tune with my subconscious. If all this starts to sound new-agey — you must remember that my eye became somewhat fixed with the 1960s because that's when I started to discover what life was about. Anyway, I think it's an image that has a lot of possible meanings. But certainly an overwhelming one is the sense of restraint and confinement — in contrast to more expansive ideas.

Q. So, David, you're not just limiting yourself to what you know you can do, but stretching yourself to go beyond, even if it's just a little.

A. I believe Degas said that "the talented does what he can, and the genius does what he must." Don't mark my words on whose quote it is — and I don't mean to imply I'm a genius which I'm certainly not — but I do want to extend and fulfill myself to the limit of what I can do, to work nearer the edge, the very boundary of my potential in the direction of what I feel I need to say.

Q. The picture, *One and Another*, has two discs that one feels one could spin and they almost, but don't quite touch. Are these also about cycles — are these beginning to imply all the thoughts that you have been using?

A. *One and Another* (the picture *Not Alone*, page 45, is similar), had a working title I wasn't happy with — it was called *Closeness*. I was trying to convey a sense of a relationship between two people. Each one of these circles represents the orbit of an independent body. Now if you were to take a point on the edge of each circle and twist the circles in toward each other — one direction to the other — the points you chose would gradually almost touch in the center. As you continue to move the discs in their paths, the points would begin to move away from each other, rotating in their circular orbits. The picture indicates to me something about the complex nature of relationships between two people. Apparently there is a coming together, and then there is a going apart — the need for separateness as well as togetherness is all part of a whole, dynamic "relationship."

Q. It seems to me extremely interesting to go through all these pieces with you. A lot of the work is about parallel experiences and it's almost as if each painting has multiple references, depending upon one's point of view. Yet the work looks so spontaneous and physical. I would be really interested to know a little bit more about how you begin to manifest these ideas — your actual working process.

A. Well, I want the pieces to look visceral and emotional and intuitive. I want them to be intuitive — but I also want them to make a kind of logical sense, a kind of sense that is extra-pictorial. I think that abstraction is always in danger of becoming merely decorative, referring only to itself. It's important for me that painting become something that has meaning, that seems to clarify, or somehow account for — or state an opinion about — experience outside of itself. I want the pictures to be emotional and I want them to be intellectual and rational too. The imagery is meant to be primal and arrived at from the subconscious, because I really believe in the Jungian, archetypal, universal experience that we all share. I would like my work to have meaning that seems emotionally revealing. The way I work, however, isn't necessarily intuitive once the initial conception — should I use the word inspiration — is realized. For example, in this drawing, which is on the theme of Descartes, which goes back to an earlier painting of this year, *Descartes' Mistake*, I actually did the drawing as a premeditated working sketch. I then executed the piece fairly consistently with reference to the drawing. That isn't the way I normally work. I tend to have more of an open dialogue with my materials. There is a kind of protracted give and take — a conversation or argument with the work. Often I get sidetracked. The work seems to be speaking back to me, the materials rather, and the discussion changes course. I end up with a painting that

seems to make sense, during the conversation at least — that seems to have meaning. But I may not have made the point that I first wanted to make. If it's a good conversation it doesn't matter if I didn't make that specific point I originally set out to make. Maybe the picture's dialog with me modified my point of view, or I lost track because the picture was talking back so much. Maybe I'll make the point another time.

Q. So in the process of making the work, you're extending the "conversation." I mean you are putting more and more psychologically and formally into the picture — and then you are getting something from making the marks and the marks are speaking back to you.

A. Yes. And these marks or images tend to be used repeatedly, like the circle or the idea of the cudgel. But hopefully each gesture and object is explored at a deeper level when I feel the need to get into that particular form — or train of thought — once again. Like this untitled drawing which is something I did between paintings. This is more intuitively arrived at, and most of my drawings are characterized by this kind of process where I simply doodle on the page with pencil — or in this case pencil and ink. Scribble with one or both hands at the same time and gradually the drawing begins to take on associative meanings on a conscious level. My consciousness tries to make sense out of the forms as they reveal themselves, and then I emphasize those lines in ink or redraw them in pencil until the forms begin to take on a kind of whole shape. These are not working drawings for particular pieces. They're simply studies, an exercise with my unconscious, trying to keep the channel open to my intuitive self, which knows a lot. It's like this whale making a beautiful sound that is truthful, that emerges once and again to reveal itself to my consciousness. Sometimes I get bits and snatches of it, and then it disappears. I often don't know what these drawings portend for future paintings, but often they anticipate images that come a year or two later.

This last piece is also very recent and returns to the image of the barrel, or circular form. It has a title I'm quite pleased with, in contrast to the previous painting. This one is called *Storage* (*Tendency to Spiral*, page 18, is similar).

I was thinking about what a barrel does. It stores material, usually liquid. There tends to be different cross-references to images I mentioned before, about the nature of them reappearing at deeper levels. It's rather like the earlier piece I showed you called *The Oracle*, except now the barrel is turned toward a hole in the wooden background framework, as though the material within the barrel is dispersing against that flat surface. Perhaps the materials being stored are thoughts, or possibly time. Certainly the potential for change and development is apparent again in this piece, as it has been in so many others. Perhaps the barrel represents a danger signal of what's being stored. The paint looks like it's leaking out from behind the picture surface. Can that which is stored be stored forever?

Q. This element of storage, are you thinking of this in a global, universal way of what the world is now containing or storing as well?

A. Well, certainly I do mean for there to be some sort of implication that involves the world situation. The beauty about abstraction though, is you can portray pure ideas without being terribly specific about them. Without having the narrative or anecdote associated with them. So at the same time there is the other possibility that what's stored is something benign.

Q. So by doing something specific and physical and direct with a container that everyone has some personal experience with — whether it's a barrel or a bucket — you can imply the ambiguity of a much more universal, global idea. And it can include all the possibilities in-between.

A. Yes, and it's something that's still hidden. I want to keep the ambiguity there. It keeps the tension there. There is a lot of ambiguity and tension about the state of the world today.

Q. Do you want to know what the oracle says?

A. Sometimes I'm tempted to peek in, but I don't know that I really want to turn that barrel around. Maybe it's better just to wait and see.

KENNETH BAKER

This essay first appeared in the exhibition catalog,
David Maxim: Paintings and Drawings. 1989.

David Maxim's work shows us how much exertion and invention it takes now to keep painting responsive to the world and to its own history without turning it topical or diaristic. Maxim makes the most objective paintings he can within the widest possible horizons of feeling and intellectual implication. Part of what they objectify (in abstract terms) is the syntactic heritage of painting as an art with a long history of materializing emotion and imaginative viewpoint. By the ways they expose their own mechanics and artistic kinship, Maxim's works enable us to note the feelings that arise when we read a painting without causing our self-consciousness about the process to deny us those feelings. You would expect exactly the opposite effect to result from building into paintings some of the apparatus used to make them.

The resurgence of image-laden art in the 1980's — a lot of it moralizing, confessional or dreamy, and most of it crowd-pleasing raised doubts about the future of abstract painting. Frank Stella pinned those doubts on the fact that abstraction can claim a history that stretches back no further than Cubism. In *Working Space*, he tries to excavate a longer ancestry of formal concerns that will yield new imperatives for the abstract painter.

But for Maxim, the impasse of abstraction today is not formal, it is the need to find sustaining purposes for — and within — painting that bypass didactics and clarify themselves through feeling, without the easy recognitions and reactions that images and canned issues elicit. The advantage of abstraction now is its capacity to delay the viewer's responses, and perhaps to de-automatize them in the process. A kind of painting that is ambiguously abstract, that is not too easily digested as abstraction, is most conductive to this possibility.

One difficulty that faces painters who work without images is that abstraction has shown itself defenseless against abuse by collectors and critics who would hijack its indeterminate significance to their own ends, for example, abstract paintings serve handily as emblems of probity for suspect institutions such as banks and other big corporations that need to shape public perceptions of their impact on society. The "autonomy" or disconnectedness of abstract art (from everything but other art) makes it ideal decoration for institutions whose stability depends in part on neutralizing curiosity about how things and events connect from vantage points of power. Thus the "purity" of classic modernist abstraction — its aloof (read: utopian) rejection of reference to mundane realities — has proved to be a liability. While the "purity" of abstraction has become a dead, merely formal, issue, its human relevance remains a live one.

Since the waning of formalist art and doctrine in the early 1970's, everyone has become more aware of ways art works can be made intractable in style and content to use as cultural merit badges. For example, Leon Golub and Philip Guston (in his last decade) have shown how imagery with a visceral edge can make paintings disquieting in ways that call attention to the works' eternal circumstances or to disparities between their intent and their presentation. Artists who use photography, performance or hybrid media — Hans Haacke and John Baldisari, for example — avail themselves of all sorts of strategies for positioning what they do tellingly against the social background. But their works, unlike good paintings, have little or not force of tradition behind them. Paradoxically, artistic tradition gains force as the public memory of life is increasingly governed by the eyeless witness to life by the official constructions of media constantly telling us that what we see and remember doesn't matter. The arts are the one area of public life that still affirm that our witness to life and our imagination for the past do matter to the world as we encounter it. As Northrop Frye points out, "The culture of the past is not only the memory of mankind, but our own buried life, and study of it leads to a recognition scene, a discovery in which we see, not our past lives, but the total cultural form of our present life." So the question now is can painting respond to the life we have in common today and evoke the depth of cultural past on which it builds, without images and without pastiche?

Maxim's recent work shows us one successful mode of reckoning with this and other current dilemmas of abstract painting. His nonfigurative paintings achieve the drama of Romantic imagery through a physical explicitness that invokes process art and the most explosive works of Abstract Expressionism.

Although free of topical references, they square with out shared sense of living through happenings of great moment whose meaning we may never know. Their overt theme is Maxim's view of creative energy as an impersonal force — a force that may even be inscrutably shaping larger events — and they are literally and emblematically devices for its expression.

About ten years ago, Maxim began experimenting without the structures that support the worked surfaces of his paintings and those that support the viewer's experience of the work as "pictorial". (These structural aspects are sometimes identical and sometimes not.) He made delicate frames of wood and fiber that tilt forward on a stretched canvas or can slide to either side of it on a narrow track. Some of them read as drawn planes that have peeled away from their grounds like sheets of mica. He also tried using more than one layer of canvas — one hung loosely against another stretched taut, for example — to keep either surface from "owning" completely the pictorial or the marginal integrity of a painting.

His tendency in all these efforts was to externalize the pictorial constituents of a painting, which had the effect of pictorializing — or theatricalizing — real space.

Since the mid-1980's, Maxim's work has had a paradoxical air of demonstrative, even violent, self-analysis. This temper is manifest in the way he paints on the reverse side of a canvas so that the strainer bars holding it taut function both pictorially and structurally. (The reversal also answers the need for external structure to support the attachments he suspends from his pictures.)

In what looks at times like satire of modernist self-reference, Maxim builds into his paintings parts of the apparatus used to make them. In *Own Other*, a relatively simple example, a canvas-swabbed slat that resembles a giant match stick is hinged and tethered to the strainerbars. It can swing horizontally to meet a small panel attached to the strainer bars. The swinging arm is caked with the ochre and citron hues percussively applied to the surface by means of it.

Giant, canvas wrapped paint sticks — "cudgels" Maxim calls them — figure in many of his works of recent years. They are tools in a literal sense and in implied narratives of process. They serve as objective pictorial forms in their own right and as metaphors for the magnitude of effort needed to make wholehearted paintings in the twilight of modernism, (Maxim emphasizes the heroic aspect of his paintings occasionally with titles, as in a series derived from *The Labors of Hercules*.)

Heroic sentiment enjoyed a kind of revival in the art of the 1980's, as invocation of tragedy in the work of Anselm Kiefer for example, and in that of Julian Schnabel, as self-promotional farce. One reason painters as different in caliber as Kiefer and Schnabel meet with large public response is that people intuit the magnitude of the symbolic stakes in creative effort of every kind, from the irreverent joke to the full length novel or wall-sized painting. As Robert Creely observed, "the heroic imagination of our time has been, of necessity, the responsibility of our artists, just that no other human conduct seemed to care that much — as long as one's own piece of the action was acknowledged and given sufficient reward." President and Plumber alike, "only work here," whereas the artist, Creely implies, feels the full implication of living here.

The heroic character of Maxim's paintings is part of their reminiscence of Abstract Expressionism. But his work manages to break free of disagreeable associations between heroic address and machismo or the imperialist politics. Maxim uses big scale, explosive paint application and big, prominent painting to try and break the limits of vision that painting inherited from "pictures". He tries to make paintings that — without images — have a visionary sweep appropriate to what we know of our place in the universe: that we are miniscule, engulfed, yet unique in our self-knowledge and the very eyes of reality as we know it. My favorite paintings by Maxim are those that evoke this paradoxical condition.

I'm thinking of *The Hunter*, a small blue-black picture with a network of white-soaked canvas nodes stretched across its surface, connected by hinged slats. The dappling of white on deep blue suggests the night sky, and the painting apparatus doubles as built-in tool and as a model constellation. In fact, the painting is based on the constellation Orion, hence its title. Other paintings hint at the immensity of the human situation (from the human vantage-point) by evoking gargantuan efforts. In *Basis*, for instance, the painting device incorporated into the work is a rope-lashed torus that rests unstably, it appears, tethered, on a shallow shelf in the middle of the picture. Some of the arcs of white and yellow on the canvas were clearly made by passes of this ungainly object. Its shape vibrates with associations to everything from blood corpuscles to UFO's to the generic wheel with its symbolism of human mind's unstoppable mobility.

Energy is the preoccupation of Maxim's art. It has taken on frightening presentiments in our age. The spectre of nuclear technology on the one hand, the depletability of non-nuclear resources on the other. The energy of invention, of the mind's very restlessness, may be the only inexhaustible resource, though it may prove to be the most Faustian and dangerous of all. Awareness of ourselves as children of energy is the fundamental recognition echoed again and again in Maxim's recent art. Perhaps that is why I see his work suffused by what I can only describe as a dark, optimistic view.

Kenneth Baker
San Francisco
December, 1989

BIOGRAPHY

1945
Born May 11 in Los Angeles; second of two children.

1962
Enters University of California at Los Angeles. Graduates with B.A. in 1966; M.A. in 1968. Both degrees are in art history.

1964
Begins to come out as homosexual

1968
Travels throughout Western Europe during the summer. Teaches art history full time at California State University, Los Angeles.

1969-70
Travels through Latin America. Paints for six months in Trujillo, Peru.

1970-76
Drops art history studies toward Ph.D. after six months at University of California at Santa Barbara. Meets Diane Johnson and Jack Murray. Decides to remain in Santa Barbara and paint "full time." Teaches part-time at the community college. Through Murray develops interest in backpacking.

1975
Mother dies. First solo gallery exhibition is at Anapamu gallery, Santa Barbara.

1976
Moves to San Francisco and meets first long-term lover, artist Ernest Posey. Meets artist Daniel Goldstein.

1978
Meets Foster and Monique Goldstrom, and begins to show regularly in their gallery in San Francisco.

1979
First significant museum exposure at Oakland Museum. Meets artists Jeff Long and Anna Valentina Murch.

1980
Becomes co-owner of the Sheet Metal Workers' Union Hall along with Ernest Posey and Daniel Goldstein. It becomes his studio and home, and is location for many artists' and gay leather community parties.

1982
Meets Walter Gorman and becomes his lover.

1984
Begins weekly figure drawing group in his studio.

1988
First of two studio exhibitions of major works at the Sheet Metal Hall studio, *The Labors of Hercules*.

1989
First solo show in New York at Foster Goldstrom Gallery

1991
First solo exhibition in Europe with Galerie Sander in Darmstadt, Germany.

1992
Participates in a studio exchange; draws for the month of June in southern France. Encouraged by friend Medardy Westrum, begins serious interest in weight training.

1994
First solo museum exhibition, Painted Philosophy. Father dies.

1995
Awarded Ludwig Vogelstein Foundation Grant. Breaks with dealer Foster Goldstrom.

1996
Because of lack of gallery exposure begins to publish his own catalogs. Vows to work on a physically smaller scale.

1998
First purchase of work by a major museum: the British Museum buys two drawings.

COLLECTIONS

Achenbach Foundation for Graphic Arts, Fine Arts Museums of San Francisco, California

Graphische Sammlung Albertina, Vienna

The British Museum, London

Brooklyn Museum of Art, New York

Carnegie Institute of Art, Pittsburgh, Pennsylvania

Center for the Arts, Vero Bach, Florida

Davenport Museum of Art, Davenport, Iowa

De Saisset Museum of Art, University of Santa Clara, Santa Clara, California

Grunwald Center for Graphic Arts, University of California, Los Angeles, California

Long Beach Museum of Art, Long Beach, California

Milwaukee Art Center, Milwaukee, Wisconsin

Museum Für Moderne Kunst, Frankfurt, Germany

Museum of Modern Art, San Francisco, California

The Nelson-Atkins Museum of Art, Kansas City, Missouri

The Oakland Museum of Art and History, Oakland, California

Santa Cruz Museum of Art and History, Santa Cruz, California

Sheldon Gallery of Art, University of Nebraska, Lincoln, Nebraska

Southern Alleghenies Museum of Art, Loretto, Pennsylvania

Sunrise Museum of Art, Charleston, West Virginia

University Art Museum , University of California, Santa Barbara, California

University of California Museums at Blackhawk, Danville, California

SELECTED SOLO EXHIBITIONS

1999
"Summer Darkness, Winter Light," Space 743, San Francisco, California
"Little Men," website exhibition. www.sirius.com/~dmax

1996
"Heroes and Giants," Space 743, San Francisco, California (catalog)

1995
"Men," Space 743, San Francisco, California; Foster Goldstrom Gallery, New York City, also: 1993, 1991, 1990 (catalog), 1989; D.P. Fong Gallery, San Jose, California

1994
"Painted Philosophy," UC Berkeley Museums at Blackhawk, Danville, California (catalog); traveling: Cabrillo Gallery, Cabrillo College, Santa Cruz, California; Sheldon gallery, University of Nebraska, Lincoln, Nebraska

1993
Thomas Gehrke Gallery, Hamburg, Germany; "David Maxim," Kunstverein, Heidenheim, Germany

1991
Galerie Sander, Darmstadt Germany (catalog)

1988
"Forum," Hamburg Kunstmesse, Hamburg, Germany

1987
"Force and Powers," The Artist's Studio, San Francisco, California

1986
"The Labors of Hercules," The Artist's Studio, San Francisco, California

1985
"David Maxim," University Art Gallery, California State University, Stanislaus, Turlock, California (brochure)

1983
Foster Goldstrom Fine Arts, San Francisco, California; also annually, 1979-1982

1979
Art Space Gallery, Los Angeles, California

1976
"Mountains, Stars, Seas and History," Santa Barbara City College Gallery, Santa Barbara, California; Plaza Gallery Bank of America Center, San Francisco, California

1975
"29,028 Ft," Anapamu Gallery, Santa Barbara, California

1998
"Drawings by Four Artists," Cabrillo Gallery, Cabrillo College, Santa Cruz, California; "Structure," Cleveland State University, Cleveland, Ohio

1997
"Recent Acquisitions," San Jose Museum of Art, San Jose, California; "Three from Amerika," Thomas Gherke Gallery, Hamburg, Germany

1993
"Private Investigations," Ops. Gallery, San Francisco, California (catalog)

1992
"The Crucifixion through the Modern eye," Hearst Art Gallery, Moraga, California (brochure)

1991
"Expressive Drawing," New York Academy of Art, New York (catalog); "Off the Wall," Sheldon Memorial Art Gallery, University of Nebraska, Lincoln, Nebraska; "Object/Context," the University Museum, Indiana University of Pennsylvania, Indiana, Pennsylvania

1990
"10 Jahre Galerie Sander," Galerie Sander, Darmstadt, Germany (catalog)

1989
"Sculpture Invitational: John Van Alstine and David Maxim," University Museum, Indiana University of Pennsylvania, Indiana, Pennsylvania (catalog); "Tradition and Innovation: 1500-1989; Recent Acquisitions of the Achenbach Foundation for Graphic Arts," California Palace of the Legion of Honor, San Francisco, California

1988
"Forum," Hamburg Kunstmesse, Hamburg, Germany; "Ten Americans," Carnegie Institute of Art, Pittsburgh, Pennsylvania (catalog)

1987
"The Artist and the Myth," Monterey Peninsula Museum of Art, Monterey, California; "Dalla Pop Art Americana Alla Nuova Figurazione," Padiglione d'Arte Contemporanea, Milano, Italy (catalog)

1986
"Abstract Dimensional Painting," Richmond Art Center, Richmond, California

1985
"Sculptural Painting," Hearst Art Gallery, Moraga, California; "Bilder Für Frankfurt," Deutschen Architekturmuseums, Frankfurt, Germany (catalog)

1984
"Artists' Choice," San Francisco Art Institute, San Francisco, California (brochure)

1982
"Forgotten Scale," Fresno Arts Center and Museum, traveling (catalog)

1979
"New Bay Area Images," Oakland Museum, Oakland, California; "Nine Points of View," Sonoma State University, Sonoma, California; "Trains, Boats, and Planes," Baxter Art Gallery, California of Technology, Pasadena, California (catalog)

1976
"Santa Barbara Selection," Santa Barbara Museum of Art, Santa Barbara, California

Anonymous. "The Arts," *The Scarlet*. Lincoln Nebraska, June 9, 1995.

___. *Bomb*. Spring 1989.

___. "The Clipboard." *Visual Arts Newsletter*, March 1989.

___. *Darmstadter Nachrichten*, May 1991, p.25.

___. "Determinism." *Lincoln Journal Star*, June 18, 1995.

___. "Die Kraft Aus dem Kosmos." *Darmstadter Echo*, April 22, 1991.

___. *Fall Gallery Calendar*. Southwest Texas State University, San Marcos, Texas, 1987.

___. "Far Out Exhibit." *Quad City Times*, Davenport, Iowa, April 12, 1988.

___. "Hercules and Antaeus." *Nike: New Art in Europe*, May 1988.

___. "Maxim Exhibit." *San Ramon Valley Times*, February 4, 1994.

___. "On the Cover." *Gallery Guide*, New York (and National), March 1989.

___. "Zwischen Orbit und Patina Kultur In Stadt Hildenheim." February 18, 1993.

Albright, Thomas. "Maxim's New Paintings: Building From the Bare Bones." *San Francisco Chronicle*, February 23, 1983.

Amann, Gloria. "David Maxim." *Cover Arts*, New York, November 1991.

Baker, Kenneth. "Achenbach's Wide Net Brings in Fine Collection." *San Francisco Chronicle*, September 17, 1989.

___. "Maxim's Stylized Violence Steals Show." *San Francisco Chronicle*, November 12, 1986.

___. "Odd Assortment of Painted Stuff." *San Francisco Chronicle*, May 31, 1988.

___. "Plan B Takes Effect." *San Francisco Chronicle*, November 26, 1993.

___. "Taking Art into Their Own Hands." *San Francisco Chronicle,* June 2, 1995.

Baron, Richard. "Art Tour." *Art/World*, Glen Head, New York, March 24, 1989.

Brunson, Jamie. "In a Hybrid Idiom." *Artweek*, March 8, 1986.

Chiapella, Julia. "Larger than Life: David Maxim's Art Cannot Be Contained." *Santa Cruz Sentinel*, November 4, 1994.

Curtis, Cathy. "Changeable Paintings." *Artweek*, March 5, 1983.

Donia, Jan."Amerika is Niet Dood: David Maxim en Het Heimwee Naar De Trojaanse Oorlog." *De Krant Op Zontag*, Amsterdam, May 12, 1991.

Eden, Peter. "Flachland mit Hugeln." *Frankfurter Rundschau.* April 20, 1991.

Ehlers-Bohling, Margaret. "Painted Philosophy Really is Neither." *Lincoln Journal Star*, July 23, 1995.

Fowler, Carol."Collector Known Art." *Contra Costa Times*, January 17, 1992.

French, Christopher. "Different Voices." *Artweek*, September 8, 1984.

Friedman, Robert. "David Maxim at Space 743." *Artweek*, August 1995.

Friedman-August, Dorothy. "Maxim's Paint Machines." *Downtown*, New York, April 8, 1992.

Gehren, Georg. "Maxim im Frankfurt." *Frankfurter Allgemeine*, March 17, 1990.

Green, Frank. "Echo-Chamber." *Free Times* (Cleveland), April 8-14, 1998.

Guenther, David. "Songs of Life." *Pittsburgh*, February 17, 1988.

Harrison, Barry. "Queer Arts Resource." Website (www.queer-arts.com), October 1996.

Hill, Shawn. "An Abstract Revival." *Bay Windows*, Boston, November 29, 1990.

Homisak, Bill. "Sculpture from Both Coasts Enlivens Kipp." *Tribune-Review*, Greenburg, PA, February 14, 1988.

___. "The Unbearable Lightness of the 'New' Abstraction." *Tribune-Review*, Greenburg, PA, February 14, 1988.

Iden Peter. "Das Richtige Suchend, Mitten im Falschen." *Frankfurter Rundschau*, March 17, 1990.

Jenkins, Steven. "The Gang of Four." *Artweek*, November 18, 1993.

Kuchinskas, Susan. "Lofty Living." *San Francisco Focus*. October 1996.

Lowry, Patricia. "Carnegie Exhibition Revives Art of Abstraction." *The Pittsburgh Press*, February 23, 1988.

Lugo, Mark-Elliot. "The View from Manhattan." *San Diego Magazine*, October 1990.

MacDonald, Robert. "Fantasies of Voyage." *Artweek*, October 6, 1979.

___. "New Images/Bay Area." *Artweek*, June 2, 1979.

Marechal-Workman, Andree. "Constructing Formal Contrasts." *Artweek,* June 5, 1982.

Marvel, William. "Critic's Choice." *Dallas Times Herald*, November 5, 1985.

Mathews, Susan. "David Maxim, San Francisco Painter." Unpublished manuscript, 1988.

Miller, Donald. "The Art of Abstraction From 'Ten Americans'". *Pittsburgh Post-Gazette*, January 29, 1988.

Neubert, George. "New Images/Bay Area." *The Oakland Museum,* May/June 1979.

Nixon, Bruce. "Critic's Choice." *Dallas Times Herald*, November 2, 1986.

Northwood, William. "Six Artists in Search of an Idiom." *The Museum of California Magazine of the Oakland Museum*, May 1979.

Redd, Chris. "Rich Folks' Treasures." *The Arts Journal*, Charlotte, February 1990.

Runge, Wolfgang. "Alles Theater." *Main-Echo*, Darmstadt, Germany. May 18, 1991

Santiago, Chiori. "Arts." *San Jose Mercury News*, March 19, 1995.

Schmidt, Martin H. "Four from America: Vier Amerikanische Kunstler und die Antike." *In Thelis*, Band 4. Manheim, 1997.

Schwalb, Harry. "Notes and Comments." *Pittsburgh*, May 1988.

Shere, Charles. "Richmond's Abstracts Explore New Dimensions." Oakland, *The Tribune*, October 21, 1986.

Stetson, Daniel. "Contemporary Icons and Explorations: The Goldstrom Family Collection." *Davenport Museum of Art Newsletter*, Davenport, Iowa, 1988.

Stutzin, Leo. "Gargantuan Struggles." *The Modesto Bee*, September 22, 1985.

Thym, Jolene. "Maxim on Canvas." Oakland, *The Tribune*, February 27, 1994.

Topiary, Samuelle. "Contemplating Queer Art II." *Bay Times*, July 1995.

Wachtmeister, Marika. "Art Frankfurt: Vasteuropa I Centrum pa Komstmassan." *Femina*, August 1990.

Wauson, Kim. "David Maxim." *Art Voices*, January/February 1981.

Webb, Barbara. "Private Investigations of Four San Francisco Artists." *Westart*, November 12, 1993.

Weeks, H.J. "Let Your Imagination Sail." *San Jose Mercury News*, November 24, 1978.

___. "Perhaps the Fabled Fleet of Agamemnon." *The Christian Science Monitor*, July 9, 1979.

Weinstein, David. "Artist Straddles the Line." *Contra Costa County, West County Times*, November 8, 1989.

Wright, Jeff. "Reviews." New York, *Cover Arts*. April 1989.

SOLO EXHIBITION CATALOGS

Danville, California. University of California at Berkeley Museums at Blackhawk. *David Maxim: Painted Philosophy*. 1994. Text by Kate Eilertsen and David Maxim.

Darmstadt, Germany. Galerie Sander. *David Maxim: Objekte und Arbeiten auf Papier*. 1991. Text by Jan Butterfield.

New York. Foster Goldstrom Gallery. Daniel Goldstein: *Reliquaries*. 1993. Text by Richard Howard, Robert Atkins, and David Maxim.

New York. Foster Goldstrom Gallery. *David Maxim: Paintings and Drawings*. 1989. Text by Andrea Schneider. Brochure.

New York: Foster Goldstrom Gallery. *David Maxim: Paintings and Drawings*. 1989. Text by Kenneth Baker and Dan Stetson.

San Francisco. Foster Goldstrom Fine Arts. *David Maxim*. 1983. Text by Kim Wauson.

San Francisco. Space 743. *David Maxim: Heroes and Giants*. 1996. Text by Nicole Blunt and Jeffrey Long.

San Francisco. *David Maxim: Drawings*. 1998. Text by Nicole Blunt.

Turlock, California. University Art Gallery, California State University, Stanislaus. *David Maxim*. 1985. Text by Hope Werness and David Maxim. Brochure

GROUP EXHIBITION CATALOGS

Darmstadt, Germany. Galerie Sander. *Zehn Jahre Galerie Sander: 1980-1990*. 1990. Text by Christiane Klein.

Davenport, Iowa. Davenport Museum of Art. *Contemporary Icons and Explorations: The Goldstrom Family Collection*. 1988. Text by Christopher Waddington and Daniel E. Stetson.

Frankfurt. Museum Für Moderne Kunst. *Bilder Für Frankfurt*. 1985. Text by Hans Hollein, Peter Iden, and Rolf Lauter.

Hamburg. Hamburg-Messe. *Forum*. 1988. Text by Ingo Von Munch, and Thomas Zaunschrim.

Indiana, Pennsylvania. The University Museum, Sutton Hall. *Graduate Art Association Exhibition*. 1991. Curated and with text by David Maxim.

Indiana, Pennsylvania. Kipp Gallery. Indiana University. *Sculpture Invitational*. 1989. Text by James Nestor.

Milan. Padiglione D'Arte Contemporanea di Milano. *Dalla Pop Art Americana Alla nuova Figurazione*. 1987. Text by Peter Iden and Rolf Lauter.

Moraga, California. Hearst Art Gallery. St. Mary's College. *The Crucifixion Through the Modern Eye*. 1992. Text by Marvin Schenck. Brochure.

Monterey, California. Monterey Peninsula Museum of Art. *The Artist and the Myth*. 1987. Text by Jo Farb Hernandez. Brochure

New York. Academy of Art. *Expressive Drawing*. 1991. Text by Elga Wimmer.

Oakland, California. The Oakland Museum. *New Images/Bay Area*. 1979. Text by George Neubert. Brochure.

Pasadena. Baxter Art Gallery, California Institute of Technology. *Trains and Boats and Planes*. 1979. Text by Michael H. Smith.

Pittsburgh. The Carnegie Museum of Art. *Ten Americans*. 1988. Text by John Caldwell.

Richmond, California. Richmond Art Center. *Abstract Dimensional Painting*. 1986. Text by Robert Tomlinson. Brochure.

San Francisco. A Plan B Presentation for Opts. Art Gallery. *Private Investigations*. 1993. Text by Eva Bovenzi, Jeff Long, David Maxim, and Joan Perlman.

INTERVIEWS

Murch, Anna Valentina. A Studio Interview with David Maxim. 1988. Audio tape. Unpublished transcription by Kim Wauson.

___. Painted Philosophy: A Tour of the Exhibition with David Maxim. 1994. Video tape in association with Walter Gorman.

McGee, Michael. Art Forum: David Maxim. Rancho Santiago College, Santa Ana, California. 1992. Video tape.

The artist thanks Anna Valentina Murch, Kenneth Baker, Nicole Blunt, William Whitehead, and Walter Gorman for their assistance with this publication. Special thanks also to Kim Wauson, who transcribed the interview.

Further information or comments:
David Maxim
E-mail: dmax@sirius.com
Website: www.sirius.com/~dmax
Phone: 415-861-7233
Fax: 415-863-1778

Anna Valentina Murch is a California-based, site-specific artist. She is also associate professor of art at Mills College in Oakland.

Kenneth Baker is art critic for the *San Francisco Chronicle*. Among numerous achievements his book, *Minimalism*, is especially noteworthy.

Nicole Blunt is a writer on contemporary art. She divides her time between her "farm" in Surrey, England, and her work-retreat in Malibu, California.